Life is an Adventure

Erin Canady-Denham

BookLeaf
Publishing

Presentation by *BookLeaf Publishing*

Web: www.bookleafpub.com

E-mail: info@bookleafpub.com

ISBN: 9789357747455

First edition 2023

I dedicate this book to my wife and son, since they have to put up with my quirkiness. Everyday is an adventure that I will always be grateful for because of the both of you.

ACKNOWLEDGEMENT

I would like to thank my mother for allowing me to go to college early. The people and experiences at SMC as well as the literature class expanded my horizons in so many ways. I also want to acknowledge my ancestors, friends, and family. My two-spirited soul would not be complete without all of you.

ACKNOWLEDGEMENT

PREFACE

Poetry is a feeling. It helps express oneself with each verse written as well as learn while reading it. We are all poets in a way. Our faces produce wrinkles and squints that others can read if they look hard enough. Our lives are an adventure... hope you enjoy reading parts of mine.

What is Faith?

Life can be so exciting,
so enthralling.
Life can be very dark,
and leaves you bawling.
What is faith in this life we live...

Plop on a chair or bed,
with no fear of falling.
Get bad news
and leave there crawling.
What is faith when we need it...

Does it give us
peace as we're growing?
Does it leave us
without knowing?
What is faith in this life we live...

Pay attention and you can see,
Children glowing
Teens unknowing
Grown-ups slowing
The elderly going
What is faith in this life we live?

The Moon...

The moon was quiet
yet so, so loud.
I could not tell yet
what I had found.
I stood to look
and it stood still.
It was so different,
and yet, so real.
The sky was painted...
a beautiful sight,
and I stood in stillness
with much fright.
Was I scared of the life the sky had shown?
Or was I afraid of being alone?
It's times like these you look at yourself,
instead of looking at everyone else.
Next time
you stop and see,
if the moon above is speaking with thee.

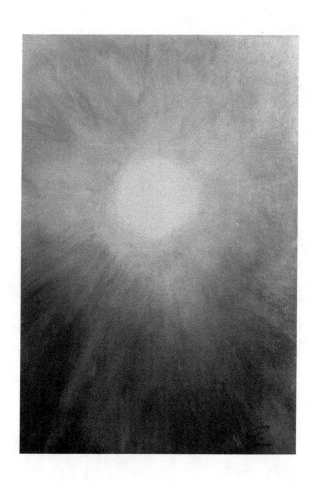

Too Deep...

A newborn baby
Oh how sweet
You kiss their hands
you kiss their feet
They grow up
get in too deep
All you do is sit and weep.

You stand and watch them from afar
with no clue of who they are
You ask yourself what went wrong
and oh it's been so, so long
since you kissed their hands
and kissed their feet.

They grew up
got in too deep
and all you do
is sit and weep.

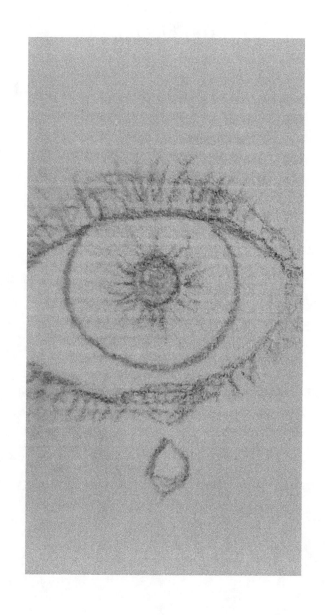

Crying...

I Hear Crying, Or Is That Rain
I See Lightning Or Is That Pain
Is He Up There Looking Down
Angry With Us, Watching Us Drown
Mad At Us For Losing Ground
No One Is Perfect...This Is True
But Is It Possible To Be So Rude?
My Eyes Will Not Stop Pouring
And Outside I Hear Him Roaring
What Do I Do, Which Way Do I Turn
Is There Something Here That I Must Learn?
I'm Not The Only One Suffering Here
Many Others Share My Tears
The One Above Is Crying Too ...
I Hear The Thunder
I See The Lightning
I Feel The Hail.

Southern girl...

Stand up straight, dress for the part.
Always smile & say bless your heart.

Scream for love...

I WORRY ABOUT THIS AND THINK
ABOUT THAT.
WILL MY HEAD BLOW UP OR MY HEART
GO FLAT?
I'VE GROWN A LOT THROUGHOUT MY
YEARS,
BUT HAVE I GROWN ENOUGH TO
CONQUER MY FEARS?
I CAN STAND BEING ALONE
BUT CAN I STAND ON MY OWN?
I AM JUST A CHILD YOU SEE
TRYING TO LIVE IN A FANTASY.
FRIENDS ARE HERE RIGHT BY MY SIDE
BUT NO ONE CAN HEAR MY CRY!
I SIGH FOR HELP AND SCREAM FOR
LOVE...

11

Shoes...

Walk a mile in my shoes if you can,
doesn't matter which brand.
You can tell a lot by a person's shoes,
it gives you so many clues.
It shows individuality,
living in make-believe or reality.
Crocs for those being comfy,
doesn't matter how much money.
Heels for those wanting attention,
and not for those in detention.
Tennis shoes for running after kids,
but not for those making bids.
Boots for those with land,
but not for the beach sand.
Walk a mile in my shoes if you can.

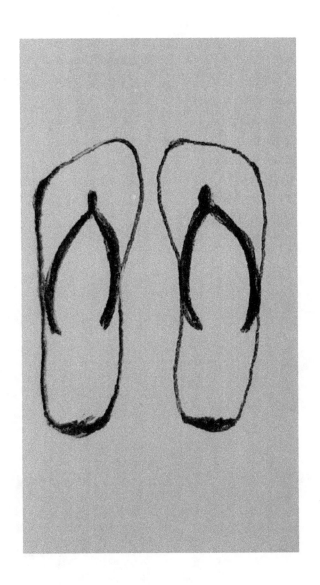

Work...

Rest is
for the weak…
so what
if you feel bleak.
Work to live
yet live to work.
Without it there's no
spoon or fork.

Life is short...

Life is short.
Paint that picture.
Buy the passport.
Write that story.
Sing the song.
Hug your family,
all day long.
Do what you love.
Love what you do.
All good things will
come to you.

So I laugh...

Life is funny,
the world is funny,
so I laugh.

Life is sad,
the world is sad,
so I cry.

What is life...

What is life
If you don't live it
What is strife
If you're not in it
What is love
If you can't feel it
What is talk
If you can't hear it
What is beauty
If you can't see it
What is life
If you don't live it

Don't give up...

Life is too short
To play it rough
Life is too tough
To give it up

My question...

I feel sorrow
I feel pain
I'm standing outside
in the falling rain
I want to talk
but no one is here
I live my life
in constant fear
What is my question
you do not know
It will never be answered
I know, I know.

This road is life...

I walk down a road,
I jump, I fall.
I get back up
to stand up tall.
I'm not afraid
of you all
I'm afraid of myself, believe it or not.
Scared of my goodness and of my faults.
Memories don't go away...
I overcome them day by day.
I walk down this road,
I sing, I cry.
Walking just to make it by.
This road is life I'm walking down
This life is something I have found
It is hard yet easy at times
And one day I'll leave it behind.

I'll hold on...

Things will still please me.
My brain will still tease me.
My pain will not ease me.

I won't give up
I won't give in
I'll hold on,
until the end.

Who's to say you didn't win…
It's all inside you my dear friend.

Life as me...

One day you'll know me for who I am.
Not for who you want me to be.
But until then,
I'll be living my life as me.

Life is an Adventure...

One worth living …
not everyday is unforgiving.
Adventures are not all the same.
This life is sometimes like a game,
and parts leave you fatigued.
Family, friends, colleagues…
Not all close to you have your back.
You pick up pieces that they lack.
Nature, home, and true love…
this is where you rest.
Adventures are the best.

Always an Adventure...

My adventure is different than yours
The big "C" word, cancer
Makes you realize that life is short
Fears I have to temper.

My adventure is different than yours
I celebrate that someone's dead
That someone hurt me
Bad dreams I always dread.

My adventure is different than yours
Came out of the closet, proud and strong
People still look and glare
Wives holding hands just wanting to belong.

My adventure is different than yours
PNW a 52-hour drive
Moved cross country
6 cats, 1 dog, 2 wives

My adventure is different than yours
Yours is different than mine
But with every adventure
You know you're alive.